SEEING IT THROUGH MY EYES

REIGH LEE

ARCHWAY
PUBLISHING

This book is a work of non-fiction. Unless otherwise noted, the author and the publisher make no explicit guarantees as to the accuracy of the information contained in this book and in some cases, names of people and places have been altered to protect their privacy.

Archway Publishing books may be ordered through booksellers or by contacting:

Archway Publishing
1663 Liberty Drive
Bloomington, IN 47403
www.archwaypublishing.com
844-669-3957

Because of the dynamic nature of the Internet, any web addresses or links contained in this book may have changed since publication and may no longer be valid. The views expressed in this work are solely those of the author and do not necessarily reflect the views of the publisher, and the publisher hereby disclaims any responsibility for them.

Any people depicted in stock imagery provided by Getty Images are models, and such images are being used for illustrative purposes only. Certain stock imagery © Getty Images.

ISBN: 978-1-6657-3404-2 (sc)
ISBN: 978-1-6657-3405-9 (e)

Library of Congress Control Number: 2022922195

Print information available on the last page.

Archway Publishing rev. date: 01/27/2023

Trigger Warning

- Some of these topics might be hard to read, because most go deep into feelings. I personally feel people do not like talking about. So, if at any point it gets hard to read, take a break from my book. The titles are what the paragraphs will be about, so that will help.

Contents

What I want to say when I hear are you okay

- When people ask if I'm okay, I laugh and say I'm fine. I want to say my depression is a battle every moment of everyday. That getting out of my bed is the hardest thing I must do every morning. I want to say that seeing my scars is a constant battle not to do it again, also a never-ending reminder about the pain I have felt. I want to say my anxiety makes it a battle to believe that after something good happens something bad won't happen after. I want to say my mind is like a train one thought comes then the next and the next, then when the train comes to a stop every thought is there and I'm thinking about a thousand different things at once. So, I start breathing fast and soon I cannot breathe. I want to say I feel like I'm on thin ice about to go under water with all my thoughts and not be able to get back up. I want to say it's so hard not to think about so many things at once, but I don't want to ruin anyone's day with my feelings. So, I keep holding back tears every day and pretend to be okay. With a "happy smile" on my face, even when I may not be. I just want someone to notice the pain I'm going through without me having to tell them or make it clear.

Can't tell if I am getting better or numb

- Honestly, I don't really feel like I'm getting better. When every time I think of things, I can't help but think about everything that has hurt me. Sometimes I cry, other times I just sit and stare into space. Instead of getting better I just do not want to think about things anymore. I push down the way I feel almost every day. Except I don't know how I feel anymore I have lost myself. I pretend to be okay every day when most days I want to break down and cry. Now a days I want to scream at the top of my lungs and let it all out. It's hard because when some-one asks if I'm okay I just say yes thank you for asking. I only say that because I don't know if I'm okay or not anymore like I can't tell if I'm getting better or becoming numb. I have always felt this way and I just can't bring myself to label it as numb. I never know how to act because I can never tell how I am feeling, and it truly sucks. There are days I just don't want to speak. Days I just want to lay in bed and go to sleep and escape all my thoughts and feelings, along with everything else. No matter what I get up every day and tell myself it's okay, you're get-ting better. I honestly don't know if that's true though, I will continue telling myself it though.

Don't remember how it feels to be okay

- When I get sad, I always think about everything that has made me feel this way and it hurts so much, I don't know how people say I like you better now that you're not depressed anymore. Depression has been a part of my life for so long so why say that. It also hurts because what if I am to me every day all I see each day as is another day of pain, that I don't know how to end. Another day I must pretend I'm okay and at night I want to cry, but no tears come out and when they do I have to be quite so no one hears me. Only because I do not want my family to ask me if I'm okay, truth is I haven't been okay. I don't even remember what it feels like anymore to be okay, and it hurts it really does. I also cannot recall the last time I was okay. How could anyone see that though I put on such a good act. So, in the end I just put a smile on my face and laugh it all away. I mean what more can I do after all I do not want anyone to know I am not okay. Why, we'll all I have to say is that I cannot help but think everyone likes me better now.

Wondering

- Is it just me, or do you ever wonder what your old personality was like. I mean like you change so much in life you forget about how you used to act around people and by yourself, just overall you can't remember. I wonder if my personality has changed for better or worse. How would I know though I can't remember what my personality was to be like to be able to tell. I wonder if people like me more than they used to back then, like which version of me did people like more. So instead, I just sit and wonder without an answer to my own thoughts.

Mad at the world

- Come on world please stop making people come into my life just to leave. I get people come into your life to teach you a lesson, but what more do I have to learn. I already live by so much since so many people have left, I do not want to keep adding onto that list. After all people leaving me is making me think I'm meant to be alone and that everyone is going to leave me. That I can't get close to anyone anymore without them just forgetting about me. You know you did me dirty by bringing someone into my life that could help me from going back into the hole that I fought so hard to get out of, only for them to leave me because now I'm falling into that hole that I don't want to fight to get out of again. If anything, I'm not planning on coming out anytime soon, so thank you world for making it so I feel I must give up. I know how it goes for me I find someone who makes me happy and then they leave me. You can't just give me someone who won't leave me for once, I haven't done anything wrong to deserve the way I have been treated. Happiness comes and goes in waves you know, in my case happiness comes in someone who just want to leave in the end. Doesn't sound very happy does it well guess what it's not it sucks it really does. It's okay though because I'm only getting used to it. Maybe the world just does not want me to be happy.

What I think a part of love means

- Love is very hard no one understands it everyone thinks they do but they don't. You can never really understand the full meaning of love, after all everyone thinks differently on things. Okay now I will write my small story, with it ending with what I think a part of love is. I got my heart broken and still can't move on from the person who broke it, even though I know I must. I really should be able to move on from him, I just can't it's so hard and I don't know why I still have feelings for them I can't explain it. My heart is broken in two and here is what both halves of my heart is feeling. One half hates him so much and doesn't want to be near him or hear his voice. The other half doesn't hate him and cares about him so much and wants to be close to him and hear his voice. It is tearing me apart and driving me insane that I don't exactly know which half to pick. I think that a part of what love is that you really don't know how you still feel about someone you used to be with, because there will always be a half of your heart that cares about them no matter what. Now you might not think that is a part of it, but I do.

A girl

- I can't remember the last time my mental health has been as good as it has been lately. My stress level has been low, I've been managing work and school good. Here is what I haven't been managing is my thoughts they are so chaotic. That I don't even know where to begin to understand them. Everything just seems so messed up and I can't even explain why. Everything I am writing down just doesn't feel right. Like normally I can put my thoughts into words so good. Now I have no idea what is even going on inside my head to write down. All I know is I am lost and have no one that I trust to try and talk to. Not that I would be able to do much talking, because how can I make them understand why I am in pain when I can't even explain to myself why I am either. I just really need someone who can help me make sense of the things I am feeling. I sure the hell don't know what I feel anymore. I don't write about God in any of the things I have ever written down, but please God if you hear me, please just give me someone I can talk to, someone who won't judge me or treat me any differently after I talk to them about things. I do not want anyone to feel pity for me. I just need everyone to continue thinking I have gotten my life together and that I am one happy girl. Even though I am a girl who has grown up too fast and has forgotten how to act like a little kid. A girl who has gone through things that hurt her more than her own words can even explain. A girl who has brought herself out of such a dark place of mind that she got buried into, because she felt she had no one to talk to and most importantly that she couldn't feel the things she felt. Why well, because she didn't have anyone there to truly support her and her emotions. A girl who is always asked what's wrong. When she acts only a bit off, but after telling them they say, "oh that doesn't even sound that bad you are just being dramatic" and she is left thinking every time if you were in my shoes, you wouldn't even be alive anymore, you would have already ended it. A girl who's always thinking she can't like the person she likes, because her friends always felt the need to say how they felt about the person themselves and for some reason it was never good things. Who knows maybe they were jealous that she was maybe just maybe close to being even the slightest bit of happy in a relationship. In the end their opinion and what they thought about the person always matter more than how I felt and my own opinion. A girl who only wants one person just one person out of everyone in the world she wants just one person to fully support her and her emotions about someone. Most importantly to just be happy for her that she might have found someone who will stick around and not just leave her. One person who would just listen and not feel the need to give their opinion about the situation. One person to look her in the eyes and tell her it's okay to feel the way you feel about this person if you are happy. That poor girl is left feeling like she will never get that one person and that she is all alone in her battle to keep fighting and stay alive. If anything, that's okay, because this girl has gotten herself through so many things and will continue to all by herself and has learned that herself is the only support, she needs about anything and everything. A girl who has also learned that she is stronger when she is alone. This girl will always want that special someone to help her out just a little and to guide her in the right direction whether that someone is a true best friend or a person she is in a strong and healthy relationship with. A girl who is left wishing that she didn't grow up as fast as she did. A girl who learned that she was by herself in this world at the age of only 12, because that is the age, she started thinking that the world was out to get her. Since that age she will continue to think that until the world gives her just the slightest bit of peace with herself and her thoughts.

Giving up work for my sport for my parents

- Every time I talk about work it becomes an argument. When all I I'm trying to do is be responsible and maybe just maybe make things a little less stressful for me. I put all my time and all I have in me into my sport. Even though I'm tired and exhausted, but when I say that my parents blame it on work. I want my winter to work, but no I am playing my sport to make my parents happy. I want to work so I can actual do what I like to do. To spend time with the people I actual want to spend time with. People who make me smile and so happy. It's not that my sport doesn't make me happy or the people I play with do not make me happy. It's that I have done it for so long that doing something new as in my job feels so good after doing the same things my whole life for so long. I didn't even want to play for a higher sports team from the start to begin with. I never complained instead I just did it like I know I basically signed up for at the start of starting to play, but I also signed up for work which my parents cannot understand. I know they want my sport to be my responsibility and priority, but what they forgot is I am also responsible for working. I signed up for that before I did my sport this year. I hardly work and that is not a point of a job to me at least. You're welcome for giving up on myself and work for my sport.

I did it for you

- I give up the one thing that I really enjoy doing for you guys. Just to do the one thing you want me to do without even realizing that maybe I don't want to do it anymore. That maybe I just want a break from my sport so that the joy I once had for it comes back, but no it's all-season round. Any time I even try to talk about changing my work schedule it becomes an argument and I suddenly have an attitude. Like no I'm sorry I get a tone in my voice, because the thought of giving up even my hours for my job for my sport and other stuff hurts. I'm sorry I'm trying to be responsible and manage everything all at once. Even though I am still young life should not be this stressful and time consuming for me I should have time to hang out with friends and go places with people, but no I give you all my energy that I have left to do stuff you want me to do. I can no longer tell who I am. Work was the one thing holding me together because it gave me no time to think about things, which yes is not completely good, but it was good for me. Anyways I hardly have that anymore, yet I literally say to you that I'm tired, I'm exhausted and I'm sore and I need a break then you have the audacity to say maybe you should take time off work. How do you even sound right, because works so the problem. No, it's softball. This writing was from a while ago and if anything, I see now I should not have worked as much as I did at a young age. So, in the end they were only trying to do what was best for me even though I thought at the time that it was working.

You must be willing to be happy

- Though I don't believe that I can truly be happy with where I am in life and what I have. I only know that you can be truly happy in life if you are willing to allow yourself to be. Also, that you can truly be grateful for what you have, if you know the reason behind why you have it and how it helps you. For me I have learned that what I have in life so far is what keeps me going and living life how it is supposed to be lived. Even though it gets completely and utterly stressful, it also brings me joy. Though sometime people can get tired of the stuff they enjoy doing, not because they don't like it anymore, but they have done it so many times and put so much time into it that it starts to feel like the same day repeatedly. No one likes feeling like they are living the same day every day, but every new day has something new to offer. Whether it brings you happiness, sadness, make you angry or numb. Any emotion, at all really. You get to choose how you feel about things so always try your best to look at things in a way no one else will understand but you.

Don't really believe in love

- I do not completely believe in love, but I believe in the concept of it. I know that doesn't make sense so let me explain it. Now I am not explaining the type of love you say to family or friends. I am explaining what I think the meaning of saying it to your current partner is. Let's start off with, love is a strong word you say to someone you truly and deeply care about in a way that words can't explain. Love has so many meanings behind it, which is why people use it so much. The biggest meaning to love to me is you say it to people you know you yourself will not leave them. I think the person you say it too, should not say it back if they don't know if they are going to stick around or not. Though that's not all that it means, I also think it is the start to something much stronger than friendship. To a new beginning in your relationship, a step closer to being with each other forever. Even if you and your partner say I love you that does not mean they are to stay with you forever, but it does mean they care about you in different ways then other people. Love can also be thrown around by people who care so little about it. When you meet your soulmate, you will know at least, I think. Because you should not be in no hurry to rush things take your time to enjoy the little moments with them. Enjoy those small talk as well. Those little smiles you get from them. Those jokes they make to pick on you because they think it's cute to see you irritated. Overall, always enjoy those small moments in life with them that make you smile.

Push people away

- Why when things start to get good for me everything turns out bad. I try so hard to believe I found happiness. Then I feel it slowly getting ripped away from me piece by piece, until all that happiness is gone, and I fall into a bad state of mind. Which makes it feel like all my burdens and problems are on my shoulders weighing me down. It's like as soon as I get rid of them, they come back ten times worse and it's not just them there is more. Why do I feel like I can never be happy, am I just not enough. Do I not deserve to be because if that's the case then why did God create me. Why am I still alive and breathing. Why create someone that everyone sees as beautiful, kind and caring. Along with too nice and plenty more things. When I can't see it myself. Why give everyone the idea that they would be lucky to be in a relationship with me, but I can't feel that way when I hear it. Because to me any guy would be ruined, no one can handle me I'm a handful I have problems after problems and I can't fix them, I also do not have it in me. My burdens and problems are a part of me they make me who I am. I have days where I won't talk, and I distance myself from those who care about me. I push those closest to me away tell they leave so I don't have to, but after they leave, I feel regret for giving them no choice. Is that what I am supposed to do push those closest to me away. Either that or am I supposed to make everyone happy and truly care about themselves only for me to be forgotten after I do so. Everyone I ever try and talk to after allowing them to stay, instead of just pushing them away like the rest they just end up not talking to me for what because you couldn't handle me or you didn't really plan on staying, after someone leaves that I thought might stay that's how I feel. Then I regret not pushing them away like everyone else I did. If you don't want to stay and want to leave me, then say that don't leave me without any reason or out of the blue. I have had so many people leave me for days then come back like nothing ever happened because they know I will let them come back, only because I didn't make them leave, they did that all by themselves. People tend to treat me like an option or use me when they have no one else or need entertainment, that's because I'm too nice and always look for the good in people to see that's what they are doing. If anything, I am starting to struggle again and I feel there is not a thing I can do to stop it this time. I get a feeling of love for myself only to have every piece of me end up hating myself. No one can tell the difference when I'm happy or sad, because the truth is no one really knows the real me. I don't even know the real me and I'm afraid I never will. That right there is my biggest fear not losing myself, but never knowing the real me. That why I just push people away, because them leaving without me doing that just makes me not know me even more.

Done with people

- I give respect to everyone and for what to get none back. People say to me you're too nice to be mean, yeah we'll watch me. If anything, I'm not scared to be mean to people who deserve it anymore and watch me learn to fight back. Everyone leaves me so why keep thinking they will stay right. So let me believe they will leave so I can make them see that I don't care anymore or make them feel bad for whatever they did to make me be mean to them whatever one works not going to lie. I can't stand people I'm so nice and try my best to make everyone's life better, but no one does the same for me. The ones who do that thank the lord because you are rare in my life. If anything, you will eventually leave, and I know that much. Expect disappointment so you don't get disappointed that's my rule for now on. I'm sorry I act the way I do now but it's because I'm building a wall around my soul for the good of me not everyone else anymore. I hurt you then I'm sorry but I'm so sick of people hurting me and I don't ever hurt them. I used to think of revenge as kill them with kindness nope I'm so done with being kind to those who have changed me, told me lies, told me what I want to hear to make me stay. Which it works but no I'm not staying for anyone anymore so have fun making me like you after you do something to hurt me. I promise you it's not going to work. I hate being manipulated by those close to me, so I won't put up with that stuff no more, or anything else that hurts me.

If you leave and want to come back into my life

- I'm tired of hearing I won't leave, then you leave like don't tell me that unless you know you mean it or if you will not prove it to me. I rather be told the truth than you tell me what you know I want to hear. After all I get tired of people lying to me. I mean I'm used to it, but still. If you say you won't leave me than please just don't. Say you do then I will not be the first one to reach out again. I will not say sorry for acting how I did after you left because I have every right to. You will reach out first and your apology better be good. If anything, I give second chances only if you are lucky though. Also, if your apology was believable and good enough to me. Along with the amount of time it took you to reach out to me again. We are not going to talk in person like nothing ever happened though because that's not fair to me and how it gets to work. If you decide to leave then do the part in forgetting me, trust me if you don't I will. So, let's hope you do first or reach out before I decide to give up and forget about you.

I don't feel like me

- I don't see myself as me anymore. Like I'm here in this world but I'm not here and it's driving me insane. I'm okay but I'm not okay in away. I feel so lost in more way than not feeling like myself. My emotions are not there anymore I feel absolutely nothing. I don't want to talk to anyone, and I mean no one. I just want everyone to leave me alone so I can go quiet, if that make sense. I mean I'm tired of peoples lies and broken promises. I'm tired of people leaving when they tell me so many times, they will never do that to me and then they do. I keep waiting for the people who left to reach out and they don't, I mean why would they. Whatever they left for they saw as good enough to leave me even if I did not. So, since they do not reach out, I want to, but I can't because that's not fair and I will only hurt myself doing so. Along with lose me even more than I already have, and I don't want that.

Can't do this

- Being around people and trying to have fun or not be boring or quiet and seem like I'm not okay, is way harder than it should be on me. I'm just the type who wants to be left alone and by myself because I have been alone for too long, I don't want it any other way at this point in my life. I don't want people to leave any more like I can't take people leaving. So many people have left and the next who does will more than likely break me. I cannot allow myself to break my own heart anymore that's not how it's going to go. I can't if I do, I will be so disappointed in myself. I broke myself with high hopes way too many times already and after my experience with one guy. I just don't know any more a relationship does not seem like it's in play for me. Also like it will not work they just leave and break my heart into more pieces than it already is. I do that all on my own with my high hopes. I can't do anymore relationships I'm going to break my heart way more than it has been if I do so.

Work

- Being at work once brought me so much joy and it no longer brings me it. Which makes me so mad that it no longer gives me that spark it used to when I got there. Now I'm stressed out and can't handle the pressure they give me. The pressure of feeling like I must be good at it. Better than anyone because that's how it seems, no matter who falls behind they tell me to catch them up making it, so I fall behind and must catch up on my own position. I used to be so talkative and smiley now I'm the opposite not talkative and I do not smile as much. Work was a safe place from stress and now it seems that's all it is causing me. I feel as though there is nothing, I can do to make it not stressful. I cannot leave a place that once brought me so much joy because I will have the hope it will bring me the same joy it used to back then. I also refuse to leave the people; they all have helped me mentally so much and they don't even know that.

If I don't know

- Being tried but still trying to do what is best for you in your own little world is the worst. Why well because you know it's not good for you and that it is stressing you out, but you do it anyways. You have this thought that if you do it more you will learn to deal with the stress, and it won't matter. I'm so tried in a way I have never felt not mentally physically but tried I've found out that, that is the worst kind of tried. I'm stuck in some way I cannot even begin to explain. I also don't know how to get out of this mood I am in which also sucks because like how can I fix it if I don't know how. I feel like I am losing myself, I don't even know me anymore. Me isn't me I'm losing me and there is nothing I can do to stop it.

Kindness gets taken advantage of

- My kindness gets taken advantage of all the time. My inability to say no I don't want to do that or just no in general. Not being able to speak my mind. Always going with the flow. It all gets taken advantage of and I'm so done. I can't take it anymore. The thing is I cannot, not be kind because I have been hurt in so many ways by people being unkind I will not, and I mean not hurt anyone in anyways people have hurt me if there is anything I can do to not do so I will. Even if it means being too kind, if anything some people need that someone to be really kind to them and I will be that person to everyone. When I was going through a tough time mentally, I wished I had someone who was way to kind. So, I will do that for people because you never know what they are going through. In the end though I only get taken advantage of for my kindness. It's okay because I'm helping them in some way, I know that much and that's what keeps me being to kind.

Ticking time bomb

- I feel as though I am a ticking time bomb just waiting to go off. Like there is nothing I can do to stop it from going off. I feel like a complete and utter burdens to those around me. I can watch out for myself, but others always try to bud in. Nothing seems to be getting better it only seems to be getting worse. I'm not trying to hurt others well I'm hurting but that's all I seem to be doing. Why is it I can't just hurt myself without hurting others in the process. This ticking time bomb inside me is taking over my life tick by tick. Everyday it's a battle and it's winning on day at a time. I'm not sure I can fight it for much longer. Pretty soon I'm going to have to give up. In the end the bomb will go off, that bomb is me.

It is all just a lie

- Why is it so many people call me cute, hot, gorgeous, pretty, etc. Along with anyone would be lucky to have you. Also, I'm surprised you don't have a boyfriend. I don't have a boyfriend because every time I talk to someone they leave. They use me, tell they find someone else. It's funny because sometime it's those who said anyone would be lucky to have me. Well then you are lucky because you almost had me, but you didn't choose me. For once I want to hear someone say all those things and stay. Like seriously that's all I'm asking for and that's all I have ever been asking for. In the end though I know it's never going to be me. That's why I put my walls up and make it so hard for them to get them down. It's funny though as well because when they do get them down, they leave. Making me put those once put-up walls even higher. All I have to say is I want people to stop coming into my life and putting up an act, tearing my walls down. Only to leave once they're done. The real question is am I really someone that someone would consider lucky to have, or it is all just a lie.

Never ending spinning hurricane in my mind

- I love how no matter how hard I try and fall asleep I can't. It's like my mind is going a thousand miles per hour and it just won't stop. All my thoughts come at me like a hurricane. I can't stop moving around, can't get comfortable. Like why I just want to have nights of peace and comfortable. Instead, it's not even close to peaceful and not comforting at all. Some nights I just don't want to sleep because I need to let the hurricane stop spinning. I want to sleep so I have energy in the morning to do stuff. But no, I end up sleeping tell two in the morning on days I don't have anything going on. The days I have stuff going on I'm so tried I don't even want to get up. I really wish I could fall asleep at night instead of having a hurricane that never stop spinning going on in my mind. I try and think of a fake scenario in my head to fall asleep to and that doesn't even work. Because some way or another I start stressing about what scenario I'm coming up with. I just can't with this anymore ever night I'm up so late, for what. Because all it does is stress me out, so I want it to stop I want to be able to sleep and the hurricane going on in my mind to just be gone.

Story no one will tell

- You ever wonder why someone is the way they are. Do you judge them, if so don't. Everyone has a story about how they became who they are today. That story is something you will never know the whole story about, or you will never hear about it at all. Because it's a story of something they feel they created. They feel as though they did it to themselves not the people involved in the story. Those stories are the worst, they eat the person holding it in apart. That person let themselves down the moment they gave into the thought that it is their fault for becoming who they are now. No one makes themselves who they are, other people will always play apart. How you chose to let them is how you become who you are, or possibly who you want to be. Never judge a book by its cover you know. People need to start listening to that about other people. Those who seem the rudest and so much more, are the people who need someone to tell the full story to about how they are the way they are. To tell someone they feel it is all their fault that they are the person they have become. When it is those who played a part in the story that make you who you are as well, not just you who makes you who you are. The story is your life. One day I hope everyone finds that someone to tell the full story to even me.

The world

- She thought the hole in her heart was never going to be whole again. Tell the world gave her everything she needed for it to be whole again. The world sent her people and put her on the right path to make her happy again, in the way she thought she never could be. Though the world still sends her tough times, instead of seeing them as why would the world do this to me. She sees them as the world is testing her and she is going to win and only learn more things she needs to know in the end. She now says you have to be willing to see the good in what the world has to offer, before you see the bad to make it through life.

Curve ball in life

- Life is starting to throw curve balls and they are hitting hard. One second, I am feeling the best I have ever felt, then next I am falling and there is nothing I can do to stop it. Too much is going on in my head my mind is racing ever thought is trying to win, which one is going to consume me. The demons inside me are coming out and I am fighting everything in me to stop them. My smile is starting to fight to never come back, but no matter what I am going to win and put a fake smile on and wear a mask to hide the pain I am feeling. No one can see me at my worst, because if they do, they will see the person they all thought they knew doesn't even know herself. If I had to say so myself that would be one curve ball in life for me and those around me If they see me at my worst.

Numb to love

- I'm numb to love, like I crave it but as soon as I get it, I deny it and don't want it. I'm numb to the fact that anyone could stay. I feel nothing more than friendship with people to protect myself. People say they forgot what it feels like to love. Well, I forgot what it feels like to love someone. I sabotage everything. I don't let anyone in even those who seem worth it and could be so good to me. I don't let them in because why would I do that to myself. Why would I spend every day worrying they are going to leave me, I am going to screw it up, I'm not going to be worth it in the end, along with so much more. I refuse to let my mind feel that kind of pain and agony. I refuse to bury my heart into a hole, or let it be broken into more piece than it already is. I hate myself for it really, I do but I know some day my heart will open up to someone and I will no longer feel numb to love, so I wait. I will wait for my mind to shut up, my heart to feel whole and myself to remember what it feels like to love someone.

Waves after waves

- The battle I once fought so hard to get out of and succeed is back. Everything I got through is all coming flooding back. The pain and agony and suffering is coming back and in waves. I'm drowning trying to stay on top of them, but they keep pulling me back under. Just when I think I got back up another wave comes, then another and another, you get the point. Anyways I want to be able to come back up and see nothing but clear and a sunny ocean. Instead, I get back up and still see darkness and rain along with nothing but an ocean full of waves. Coming at me to drown me and never let me win. The waves are my battle, and I am trying to win, and I just keep losing.

I will live my life

- I have such a heart of gold, and it seems like even though I do I'll never win. I always hear you're too nice. Yes, I know that now are you going to be one of those people who take advantage of my kindness or just accept it. I always hear she doesn't hate anyone, you're right I don't. Though someone people I could. I refuse to live life hating people. Yes, you screwed me over or hurt me but that's what people do, real question is are you going to make up for it, do it again, or we both move on from it. I know I'm too nice sometimes and my kindness runs deep. Only because I will never, and I mean never hurt anyone in the way I have been hurt. I will never make anyone go through what others have put me through. I will live my life trying to do good. I will live it trying to make others happy and lift there breaking souls into light. I will live my life bringing people the comfort no one ever gave me. I will live my life listening to what others have to say so I can help them through it. I will live my life bringing nothing but kindness to this world. Because everyone no matter how much shit they have done or what type of person they have become they still deserve kindness. Everyone deserves a chance at happiness and that one person who is willing to give it to them no matter what. I say this world need more people with empathy and a heart of gold, I have learned that.

Dig a grave for me to walk past

- I give nothing but kindness to this world and those in it. Only to get manipulated, used, betrayed, and hurt. Well, I am left with a grave that they dug for me. I'm too nice I walk right around it and go right back to them even though they showed me I mean nothing to them, except for someone they can dig a grave for and know they will see right past it and come right back. It is not the fact I saw past the grave; it is that I chose to ignore it. Why you ask, well because I could be someone people want to dig a grave for and still try my best to make them see they need me. Even when they showed me that they don't.

Depression

- Here we go again falling into the spot I fought so hard to stay out of. The best word I can use for how I feel is numb. Like I don't know why that is how I feel, because I'm happy but I'm not happy. I want to scream at the top of my lungs so I can finally hear myself and let it all out. When I feel that I know that it is getting bad again, I want to cry but no tears come out. The smile that covers my pain hurts to make. I don't know why I'm feeling this way again I mean hey it comes and goes in waves they say. So let me say this I hope this wave goes away fast because I don't want to drown in it all over again. I want to be able to see the light through it all. Though all I can say I see now is darkness. I have not written about my depression in a long time but I'm going to. I have a mask on my face and only I know that it is fake. The laugh I make is not genuine it's all a lie. The smile you see is nothing but a disguise. I don't know what to think of things anymore, everything just seems so dumb. Like all that I am doing feels like it is for nothing. Everything I have fought so hard to hold onto feels like it was all for nothing. The biggest thing I tried to hold onto was myself, doing so I lost myself. Proving it was all for nothing. If I can't even hold onto myself, how am I supposed to hold onto anything or anyone else.

Fighting everything in me to stay

- See I finally get into a relationship after saying no to everyone, because I was scared to give anyone, and I mean anyone a chance. Anyways I decided to not let my emotions cloud my judgment and ruin my chances. So, I decided I would date someone again and right now I am. Some days I do not feel like they will leave me the others it is all I think about. I'm scared because I want to be good enough. I want to feel like in the end it is all going to be worth it. Instead, I'm drowning in the fact that I am no longer single, that I have someone to call mine and someone who calls me theirs and overall, I just do not know what to think about it. I'm excited don't get me wrong but I feel as though I am better off when I am alone. Now I am fighting everything in me that's telling me leave him and continue to do this on your own and get through this alone. Because for some reason instead of my depression getting better since getting into this relationship it is getting worse and it scares me, because I do not understand why.

Waves

- Yeah, it is back. That feeling of falling into the dark place, I fought so hard to stay out of and have been fighting so hard not to feel like I am falling back into it is back. It is amazing how I get waves of happiness but the waves of bad ruin the good ones. Each wave gets bigger and bigger as the days go on. I haven't felt a moment of the waves being calm, since you left me. Come on, I hate myself for it, but I cannot be talking to someone after you left. Here I am though talking to someone, and it is taking everything in me to act happy about it, because deep down I know that I should be he is a good guy after all. I can't hurt him and tell him I can't do this. Because I know how it feels, I'm so good at putting other people's feelings before my own and losing myself in doing so. I don't know what to do or who to talk to about this. I only have myself, I've only had myself for so long I'm just used to giving myself advice and never taking it. If I can't take my own advice, how can I begin to take other peoples. I just want theses waves to calm down.

You met my expectations

- You know it is great having someone like you with me. Being able to talk to someone so respectful and caring and overall, just amazing, as you. I have never had someone like you in my life. Like I have been asking and asking for someone to see me as one in a million and you said I am one in a trillion. That is even more than I was asking to be seen as. I have put up so many walls and put up so many expectations for a guy. So far you have met every single one of them. Even the ones I said I could never find. You are the guy I have been looking for. I just find it so hard to believe I got it. I just feel like everything is all so much all at once. As I said I have never had someone like you in my life and because of that, I have honestly no idea how to truly feel about it. I have only ever had guys who gave me be minimum and I was okay with it because I'm just laid back. You have given me so much more than bare minimum it is unbelievable and comforting. I just don't know with getting broken up with not that long ago, I'm not ready for anything at all. Even a talking stage, but I won't let me not completely being ready stop me, from having a taking stage with you. I refuse to let you go because I know you could be the best thing to ever happen to me. So, I will be ready for you soon it is just so hard now. You have met my expectations. So, in the end there will be a you and me.

No longer me

- Well shit, the world around me doesn't even feel real. I feel like I'm not here alive and living, walking and breathing. When I know I am doing all that, but it just doesn't feel like it. I'm losing myself I'm going down in a spiral. Which to me is okay because guess what I'm handling my shit all on my own. Maybe not in the best way but I'm doing it, I'm still here. Even though every day is a battle to just keep going and not fuck up even more than I have been for the past weeks. Every day since he left, I won't even lie I just think whatever happens to me happens, fuck I don't care, I've been through worse. Him leaving after I decided to let him in, after me never letting someone in hurt. Along with him having the audacity to say he knows how this will affect me and make the breakup a bunch of lies, is bullshit and fucking hurts. Like come on, I lost myself when I lost you. I'm not me anymore fuck I don't even know who me is. I'm gone, and I don't want to be here. I won't even lie, but I have made it this far acting strong and getting myself through it, I will continue to get myself through it. I just know that I no longer can handle this world and I just want to be alone and by myself. Alone where no one can see me, talk to me, or somewhere no one knows me a fresh start. I'm done. I don't know what to do, I don't know what to say, I just can't. I've lost myself worse than I ever have before. With doing so I have started to fuck my life up and I don't care to stop my actions from getting worse. Fuck it you only live once.

What took me from you

- Yeah, lucky me, I get depression and anxiety from a bad relationship that ended tough and continued to be tough even when it was over though that was kind of my fault still. I get mental illness from getting into things people are supposed to in life and those things changed everything for me. I mean everything from how I saw the world to how I act. Those illness took everything from me. So, after that bad relationship I got into so many just trying to forget the one who hurt me. I will say it never really worked; it was all just a distraction from how I truly felt. After a bit I saw that and went three years single never daring to let anyone in, because I knew if I did, they would just leave me in two weeks and hurt me in the end. Anyways I got into one right before I almost hit three years being single. I thought that it was a good relationship. I didn't think it would end in two weeks otherwise I would've never let him in, well shit because it did and it hurt, it hurt a lot. What I have been protecting myself from for so long happened and I couldn't handle it. This time it took everything from me it took reality from me, it took the feeling of the world being real from me. I went to the hospital and got diagnosed with depersonalization and derealization disorder. After finally letting someone in after so long I ended up losing myself more than I ever could imagine. My trust has been broken and I have lost me.

Depersonalization and Derealization

- Reality doesn't feel like reality. I feel like I'm not here in this world, when I know I am I just can't feel it. Things don't feel real. I feel like the world around me is either moving fast or very slowly. The sounds around me are very loud if they are not then they are very quiet. I can either feel my hands and not feel like I am in control of them, or I can't feel my hands, but I know I am in control. When I look at my phone it's like the only thing around me. At times I feel as though I can't even feel my own hands, or like I'm not actually touching them, when I know I am. I feel very slow like my movement are ten times slower than they normally are. Distortion in time, distance and sound. I feel emotional or physical numbness to the world around me. Sometimes I feel like I am not in control of my speech and movement. But I know I am I just can't feel it.

Restless nights

- You can't sleep because so many things go through your head, and you just can't stop moving. You're tried just not tried enough to sleep you close your eyes, but you cannot fall asleep. Your mind for some odd reason just wants to think about everything at night at it becomes so restless causing you to have a restless night, you have the urge to do something anything I mean anything to have your mind become not so restless, so you can sleep. What is there to do at night, nothing so you just try your best to sleep, and it doesn't work. If you get close to falling asleep you have some urge to open your eyes, making it so you are even more awake. You will sit on your phone and do random things or turn the TV on and watch a movie, in hopes of making yourself more tried. Truth is if you are restless that will not work. When you have a restless night all you really can do is hope your body and mind become tried and realize you need sleep.

Words hurt

- What the fuck is it that someone can say such hurtful things, not even thinking about how badly it will hurt the other person. Why is it that no one understand anymore that words hurt. Do they not understand that words have the power to change someone completely. That words can be very hard to forget. People no longer understand the power of words. They no longer care to think before they speak. People just say what they think even if it can be hurtful to the other person to read/hear. Did people forget there is a saying that goes "Sticks and stones my break our bones but words will break our hearts." Because it is true words can build people up or tear them down. It is not that hard to put other people's emotions and feelings into mind. You want people to do that for you, but why can't you do it for them. Do people do not remember to treat others how you want to be treated. I don't see people doing that anymore in this world. People don't remember how to treat other anymore. When it is not even that hard to put what you say, before you say it into mind. It is not that hard to treat those around you how you want to be treated either. In the end though words can cut deeper than a knife.

Forgiver

- She was a forgiver. She has a heart so big; she always forgave people too easily no matter what. She never knew how to give up on people. She never knew how not to forgive; I mean after all she always thought everyone deserve forgiveness. People make mistake and they learn from them, even if they make the same mistake repeatedly. She always looks for the good in the people she cares about, more then she should ever time. It was until she got walked on so many times. She had no choice but to let go of those who burned holes in her heart.

Fire

- A fire is used when someone is cold so they can make themselves warmer, but when they are all done with the fire, they put it out. Just like someone who is trying to make themselves feel better they use people. After they feel better than no longer need the person, they were using so then they put them out, meaning they leave them. Just like a fire after you put it out, except they always come back to use the fire again. Someone who is trying to make themselves feel better by using you will always come back to use you again. People treat me like fire always using me and coming back to do it again. If anything, a fire is bound to be put out sooner or later. People never let it stay lit. When left on it can cause them to grow and no one wants that, they put them out right before they start to grow. When someone sees a fire at its brightest, they also put them out, because why leave them on after all it only causes problems. People put fires out all the time and that stops the fire of course. A fire light always gets put out or dies in the end. What I am trying to say is life feels like a fire bound to be put out.

Without failure you can never get success

- I hate failure, it only makes me think I am not doing or giving enough. Though in the end I tried my hardest and that is all that matter. I see it as me failing is one step color to success, one step closer to getting were I want to be in life. One step closer to accomplishing what I want to accomplish. Failure is another word for mistakes, and mistakes are a part of life. You learn from them, and you only get stronger and better in the end. Failure is a risk you always have to be willing to take. If you are not afraid to take that risk and fail, then you already have a chance at success. You will never get anywhere without failure that is why without failure you can never succeed.

The tables have turned

- I see at as funny how back then when we were younger you judged me and told me I am being dramatic for feeling the way I felt about things. When now a day in life as we grow older you are feeling the same things I felt back then, oh how the tables have turned. See though I would never judge or call you any kind of rude names, only listen and be there and no matter what you have my support throughout everything you are feeling. Did you do that for me at all, no you did not but that does not mean I cannot do it for you. When I see my friends that never had my back for how I felt about things and the things I was going through. Be feeling very close to how I felt, I cannot think the tables have turned. Now it is your turn to see how I felt, after all you didn't understand it back then. There is a chance now that you can. That you most likely will. In the end the tables will always turn some way or another.

Everything I want to feel

- How I could go on and on about this topic is just sad. Starting off with in my eyes the most important, I want to feel love for myself. I want to be able to look in the mirror and not hate what I see, hate who I have become, hate what I have felt, or what I have been through for things. I want to feel happy and not like all I am doing is faking my smile, I want the smile I make to be genuine and true. I want the laugh I make to sound happy and not a lie to make people think I am having a good time. I want to feel okay with where I am at, instead of wanting to go back and change choices I have made for things. I want to feel at home with someone, I want a friend who will be there and have my back through thick and thin, bring me comfort in even the smallest of ways. I want to feel like everything I am doing is good enough and will not just be for nothing. I want to feel as though I have something to look forward to each day, not just another day for pain. I want to feel peace with my mind and heart. I want to feel no tears running down my face at night for things I know I should shed no tears on any longer, then I already have. I want to feel like no one hates me, when I know people honestly have no reason to hate me. I want to feel like I am not being judge for how I feel, because for some reason everyone always has something bad to say about how I am feeling. I want to feel good enough for someone to be with, because every time I get without someone, they only leave me in the end, making me feel not good enough. I want to feel energy not that fake kind of energy or the energy you have to force yourself to feel, the kind that comes naturally because you are in joying the moment you are in or the things you are doing. I want to feel so many things and I'm scared I never will.

It is me against the world

- Every day is a fight to keep going, I do not mean the type of keep going where you end your life. I mean the type where you keep doing the things you love and find joy in. Keep doing the things that put even the smallest of a smile on your face or make you laugh very quietly. I do keep doing those things and more because I see it as it is me against the world. I am going to have tough times that bring me down and make me feel like I have been thrown to the curb. That is life though right, no one in life doesn't go through some type of tough time. Everyone sees things differently; every one's pain is caused by different things. In the end it is everyone against the world not just me. I get the feeling it would be easier to just stop trying and fighting for things. I will not do that though because I will keep fighting this world and making the absolute best I can of things. Because in the end the world it is testing me and I am going to win, after all I feel as though it is me against the world at the end of the day.

Broken but still feeling love

- The number of times I have felt broken by so many different things tears me apart. I have been broken by myself, by friendship, by relationships, by work. Those are just some things that have broken me, there is so much more. Even though the things that have broken me tore me apart, I still feel love. Just because I am broken does not mean I cannot still love, just because people have broken me does not mean I cannot still love them. Does not mean the things that have broken me don't still have a place in my broken heart. At the end of the day, I am broken but still feeling love.

Where did we go wrong

- I tried so hard to hold and fight to not let something go wrong, but in the end it did. What happened where did we go wrong through. Did I let you down, was I not everything you wanted me to be, was I not enough. Did you find someone else, was I a backup, was I an option, or someone you wanted to play. There is so many things that could have been where we went wrong. Which sucks because unless you tell me I will never know. I think we could've worked it out and gotten through whatever it was. Sadly, though we went wrong, leaving me to constantly think where we went wrong.

I won't give up on us

- When we ended, I could not help but think there is still a chance, I can get him back I just have to fight. I tried my hardest to make you see it and it never seemed to work. So, I will wait no matter how long it takes for you to see you want me back. I will put everyone else aside and give no one else a chance, because the only one I want is you. No one will get my attention; I will wait for you because you are the only one, I want to give my attention to. If you do not come back, you will always have a place in my heart. I am not saying you need to come back and want a relationship; I am saying to come back in general. Like I am just fine with a friendship I just want you in my life. I cannot give up on someone who meant so much to me in such a little amount of time, I do not have it in me to do so. I will keep holding on I won't give up on us.

Shit happens

- You lose people, you lose yourself, you lose love, and you can lose so much more. Shit happens you know. You can try your best to not let anything happen that you do want to happen. You can try and put things aside, sooner or later you will have to deal with it though. You can try to ignore everything so nothing can happen, so nothing can break you, make you cry, tear you apart, ext. At the end of the day shit happens. Every single day something will happen or not go how you planned. The world was not made to be easy or anything close to perfect. So why would your life be, why would what you had planned be. I live by shit happens, how you chose to let it affect you is how it plays out.

Why is it always me

- People tend to blame their feelings or problems for things on me, making me feel as though I have put my trust in all the wrong faces. The thing is if blaming it on me help you go ahead. Don't talk to me about it if in the end it is going to be my fault about what you are talking about, when I had no part. Relationship never workout for me, they never do last long and somehow, I am the reason it ends. When I give everything in me to those I am with. When a friendship ends it all my fault, when we both did it. I try to fight for it to last and you do not so do not say it is my fault. Arguments always get put on me, when I am not trying to make it an argument. When something does not go as planned it is because of me, when I was not the one planning it, you were. All I am trying to say with those things is why is it always me.

Am I the problem

- Am I not good enough or did I not try hard enough. Did I not give my all or did I give too much. Was I not who you wanted me to be, because I can change. Did I do something wrong or did I say the wrong thing. Could you not handle my problems, because I never was asking you to help just listen. Was I not the one for you, is there someone else. I feel as though I am the problem like it is my fault. So, answer this for me before you leave, am I the problem. Because I would have given you my all through the thick and thin in my life if it was going to help you. I do not think there was anything wrong with me after all everything I did during the relationship was so that I could be enough to you. I mean yes there could have been, but we should have talked it out and I could have become better so that you would stay.

Just breath

- I cannot bear hearing just breath, you know what I am. If I was not, you would obviously be able to tell. Now maybe I am not breathing right but I am still breathing the best I can so do not say "Just breath." Telling me that just makes it worse. I get so angry hearing you say that, making me breath faster and worse than I was to start. I can calm myself down if I need to breath fast to do so let me. I have too much going on in my head at once to slow down. My mind is racing causing my heart to beat faster and making me breath faster. My mind needs to get through all the thoughts before I can breathe slower, you telling me "Just breath." Only puts more thoughts in my head. So, in the end do not tell me to "Just breath."

This is where it ends

- I fought for you to stay even when I know I shouldn't of. I kept telling myself it would be worth it. How is it worth it though when you caused me more pain than you did happiness. When all you did was hurt me mentally and destroy my heart. I gave you my all and you only gave me bare minimum, so why did I even think of fighting for you to stay. When deep down I knew I should have just held the door open for you. I see now it was not me that was not good enough, it was you. I see that it was not me who was the problem it was you. I tried so hard to see the good in you even after you left, that is why I was fighting to make you stay. In doing so I convinced myself that it was me who made you leave, so I thought I owned it to you, to fight to make you stay. I am no longer blind I see eyes wide open now, so this is where it ends. I am done fighting to make you stay.

Change so I am not the same girl you were with

- After you left, I felt the need to not be me. I changed me in ways I should not of just because you left. I just could not bear looking in the mirror and seeing the girl who was not enough. You made me feel that being me was not enough. Why did I let you do that it felt right for the first month after you left, then after I realized I should have stayed me and showed you exactly what you lost and choose to let go. Anyways here is to those who are reading that wonder what I changed. To start off with I dyed my hair darker, and I got more ear piercings. I changed my personality; I got quieter and became meaner. Which I knew I should not of but as I said it felt right at the time. I stopped fighting for people and trying my best at things. I became the opposite of me just so I could look in the mirror and not hurt. In the end I realized it still hurts because now I am no longer me. So, I went back to being me after a while but for a bit I changed so I was not the same girl you were with. Just so that I could cope, because I had no one to talk to about it. Since all people did was judge that I was so hurt.

Wish we didn't say goodbye

- To this day I still wish you were still a part of my life. It doesn't have to be big; I would be okay with just texting very little and never talking in person. I just want you in my life. After all I still wonder what you have been up to or how you have been feeling. I want to know if you have been doing good or bad with things. If you are happy or sad in life, along with so much more. I just wish we didn't say goodbye. You were one of the best things to happen to me during the time we had you made me smile and laugh so much. You made me overall genuinely happy with life. I wanted to wake up every day knowing I would get to talk to you, or even see you. Being around you was comforting, you made it feel like it was just you and me against the world. Now I must do it on my own, just wishing you were still a part of my life.

Poured more water

- I was drowning, and he saved me at least I thought so. He saw me at worst, and I thought he was going to help when he came into my life, turn out he was only planning on making me drown even more. I did not see that at the time of course I only realized when he left. He knew what he was doing all along, but I did not. He knew the plan was to pour more water and make me drown even more. I chose to see past all the red flags why you may ask well I was trying to find someone to help me stop drowning. Little did I know it would end as I was drowning and he proud more water.

Time machine

- Sometimes I dream of building a time machine and going back and changing things. After I wake up though I see that why would I want to do that, after all everything that went on in the past is in the past for a reason. The past made me who I am, and I wouldn't want it to change at all. Though I have to say my past tastes bitter, like when I think about it, I only seem to think about the bad things. Oddly enough that is all I can vividly remember. So that is why I dream of building a time machine. I am sure I am not the only one who dreams there was such thing as a time machine to take you back to the past or see what the future has in hold for you.

Life is like a book

- You have to choose to like the people you don't know, in order to like them when you met them. If you chose to think nothing but bad before you even get to know them, you might as well just be judging a book by its cover. You have to be willing to see the good in them and want to know more things about them, to understand and like them. Just like a book you have to see the good in the cover and be willing to read more than just a few pages to see if you like it or not. A book will be judge before you even buy or read it, just like someone's life. They will be judged you before they even know you or even get to know things about you. People are like how some people are with books, only willing to buy it if they like how it looks. Meaning some people are only willing to like someone based off how they look.

Climbing mountains

- I have endured several hard times in my life and for every one of them, I had just learned to push them down until I could bare the fact those hard times had happened. Though I can say that pushing them down never really did help. I can say everything that has happened has made me a stronger person than I could ever see today. I wouldn't change anything about it, because without it I am not me. Hard times are different for everyone. That's why nobody should ever judge anyone for what they're going through, it might be the smallest thing for you, but the biggest thing for them. I have had people say, "oh that is not that bad, I've gone through worse" or why do you even care, it is not that big of a deal." Them saying that never makes anyone's problems or reasons for hurting any better. Because of the things I have endured, and the words people always seem to have to say. I can finally say I am strong enough to overcome it all. That those problems have taught me to climb mountains.

Crave love

- I would give up anything to feel the type of love I crave. You know it sucks wanting to be loved and always being left feelings as though you were not enough. Left knowing you gave your all and they did not care. I cannot help but think love is useless and doesn't matter. That I will never get it or find it. Though I still search for it in everyone I met. I will never stop searching for and craving the love I want.

Addictions

- I hate addictions they are so hard to overcome it is so annoying. I know I should stop but I cannot. I feel as though the things I am addicted to is the one thing that is keeping me going and getting me through life. I think if I let go of my addictions then I will lose myself, that I will fall and never stop falling. I use my addictions to get through things. I mean I guess that is what an addiction is. Why did I have to get addicted to things I know are not good for me. Why did I even have to start it, I feel as though that is how anyone who is addicted to things that are not good for you feels as well.

Pills

- I started taking pills for my depression and anxiety and I cannot help but feel like they are taking apart of me. Like I know that they are supposed to help with depression and anxiety. For some reason though I am constantly over thinking that if I keep taking these pills, I will no longer be me that I will lose myself. Because I have had those mental illness for four years now. I cannot imagine myself without them, they make me who I am, and I like me. I am not ready to let go of those parts of me in fact I do not want to. I cannot help but feel depressed that I am getting two parts of me taken. Like the pills I know will not make those mental illness completely go away but they will help. Which to me is not helping because those mental illness have gotten me through life for so long. Sure I have some rough days were they are worse than ever but that is okay because I am fighting through those days and only come out stronger. These pills for my mental illness only are making me feel fake. No one seems to understand that I like the way I am without them. I've made it this far why start having me take pills now.

Won't let my walls down

- I could have the best friend or best boyfriend and I still refuse to let my walls I have around my heart completely let down. I put them there for a reason so that I wouldn't get hurt, after all I cannot recall a time where when I let them completely down it did me any good. So, I keep them up never daring to let them down fully. You will not get to tear them down only to put them up higher than they ever were like everyone else did. Now I am not saying you will but if there is a chance one day you leave at least I never let my walls down completely, to get hurt. Because no matter who it is I will always expect them to leave eventually, so that I do not get to hurt when someone leaves.

Self-harm

- I used to self-harm badly, I will not go into detail how bad. I will explain how I felt after I did. After I cut my skin, I felt relieved like some of the weight I have been carrying on my shoulder were gone. I felt at peace with my mind because I finally gave in and gave my body and mind the feeling it craved. Let me go into detail how I felt after I did it though. After I did it and the next day came, I felt regret for giving in, I felt regret for coping with whatever was going on in that way. I felt horrible as though I just made the worst mistake in my life, but the thing is when you are addicted to cutting it takes everything in you to stop. Now I will talk about how I feel being clean. Looking at my body and seeing the scars hurt, because then I remember I used to cope that way. Seeing them makes me think, I want to remember how it feels again. I chose to see my scars as good to get me through the fact I am clean. There is a saying that goes "she conquered her demons and wore her scars like wings." That right there make me feel so much better about the fact I used to cut. Because you are right, I did conquer my demons. Now I chose to wear my scars like wings and nothing else.

You did me dirty

- You fouled me you had me thinking you would stay. You had me feeling as though you were not going anywhere. That I was the only one you wanted in this world. Then you got up and left, you left me after filling my heart with lies. Leading me on and telling me the things you knew I wanted to hear until you decided that you wanted to leave now. How could you do that I rather just have you tell me the truth then some dumb lies. The truth hurts I know that but lies hurt even more. You did me dirty, you played with my heart. You made me feel as though I was enough only to show me in the end you never though that. You just wanted me to not leave you, so you could leave me when you were feeling better. You used me for attention and affection. Leaving me to feel what good, no you made me feel as though I just spent some of my life living a lie.

Good and evil side in everyone

- Everyone has a dark side, a side of them that is not good. Those who do not show it to people fear themselves. Along with strong for never letting that side come out. Everyone has a good side, now that side is the side people rather have people see. I mean I don't blame them. With good comes evil. Which is why I personally think everyone has a good and evil side. The world needs good and evil without it the world would be boring. I mean without evil everything would be nice and easy, but that is not life. Things will be hard, and things will be easy. That is just life as we know it so far.

I'm not lazy

- Everyone tells me why you are so lazy. Like no I am not lazy. I am tried, I am hurting, I am giving up and do not have it in me to do anything. Yes, I want to do something do not get me wrong, but nothing seems enjoyable anymore. Nothing makes me feel happy or makes me laugh. I only feel good when I am in my bed. Anywhere else and I am just so done. So, you can stop calling me lazy, because yes it may look that way. The thing is you can't not feel how I feel and if you did you would see why I am acting as though I am lazy.

If you were in my shoes

- If you were in my shoes back then when I was younger and feeling all sort of emotions and had no one to talk to, because everyone would just be so quick to judge me. You would have given up. You would have just been done. So please do not say "Oh I get it" or "I know how that feels like." Yes, I know you are just trying to be nice but me and you both know you do not understand, and you never will unless you were in my shoes. If anything, yes you might get it a bit, just do not act as though you completely understand. After all it is my life not yours so you will never completely understand even if I tell you about it and go into as much details as I can.

This is harder than I thought

- I personally love writing down my feelings but at times it is way harder than I thought it could be. Like I have so much I want to say, but I do not even know where to begin. So, I start rambling on nonsense. I go back and read it and think oh that does not sound that bad or that is actually a pretty good start. So, I keep rambling on and slowly but surely it all comes together, and I think to myself okay that was not bad. Either way sometimes it seems way harder than I thought it would be. I guess I just need to slow my mind down at times and just start with what I am thinking and write it down, because I personally feel that normally gets me somewhere with what I am writing down about my feelings.

I don't get it

- Why is sometimes I go everyday with writing how I feel, then other times I go days without writing. It makes me mad in a way, because like I love writing how I feel. I could go on and on about how I feel but for some reason there are times I feel nothing. So, I have nothing to write about. If I wrote every time how I feel nothing and wanted to write but I did not because I feel nothing. You honestly would never hear the end of it. What I am trying to say is I don't get it I love writing, but I cannot write unless I am going through something, or something just happened, and I want to write. It does not even have to be about what I am going through or what happened just a random subject, because to me it always helps. I hate it when I can go on and on about something I am writing then other times I can only get a few words out. Guess certain things I am writing about just means more to me, that I feel more towards it.

The lake

- When I see a lake, I think it is more peaceful than I ever will be and then I remember it may look peaceful, but underneath the surface. There is so much going on, that we do not see. Just like in someone's life. People have things going on that you cannot see, under their smile and laugh. Just like a lake you cannot feel how it feels unless you are a part of it. As in someone's life you cannot feel how it feels unless you are living their life. Even in a lake everything in it feels something different. Just like people in this world everyone feels something different. Never judge someone by the way they come off, because there are things that you cannot see underneath their surface.

They don't realize

- I do not think anyone realized how long I had to fight to be living my life. Seeing things at its best and not feeling pain every day. How many days it took everything in me to just get out of bed. How many days I tried to use music to out tune the world, everyone and everything in it. I do not think anyone realized that my smile was not true to myself nor was my laugh. They did not realize I was filled with agony, pain, and regret. They did not realize everything they saw as so little in my life was the biggest in my eyes. No one could see I did not like the way I looked, or how I felt when I looked in the mirror. They did not realize I stopped liking who I am a long time ago.

If you asked me how I am doing

- I would lie and say I'm fine. I would lie and say that you are not on my mind anymore. Only because I refuse to let you know how I am truly feeling. I would lie and say that I have forgot all are small memories. That I no longer think of you late at night when everything is silent. I would want to tell you how every time I close my eyes, I start thinking of what we could have been if you did not leave, but I won't admit that. I would lie and say that every time I hear someone say your name, I don't start listening to hear what they are saying. I would lie and say that I wouldn't give up the whole world for you to be in my life again. The lies I would tell you just so you do not get to see how I really feel.

Haven't I given enough

- I gave you my all, everything I had left in me, and I still wasn't enough. I put all my energy and time into us, but it still did not work out. I told my friends and family about you, for what. I helped you with your problems, I gave you advice and was by your side through everything. Even though I was dealing with my own things. I was a shoulder for you to lean on after a long day, I was arms to hold you when you needed it most. I stayed up late at night when you couldn't fall asleep so you would have someone to talk to. I left my ringer on the nights I did not stay up with you and the nights I did, in case you needed me. I made myself look like a fool when I could see that you needed a smile or laugh. I did so much for you, that seemed like you saw it as so little in the end.

Never knew a hart could break itself

- I loved you in a way I never knew I could. I let you in after never letting anyone in for so long. I gave you a chance when I knew it would come to an end, never did I think it would've ended so fast though. I trusted you with my problems only for you to tell someone after you left me that the real reason you left me is because you did not want to deal with my problems. I gave my all after never giving anyone anything. I fought myself to stay, instead of leaving when for some reason my mind kept telling me you are better off alone. In the end I never knew a heart could break itself. I did it all on my own letting you in. With the feelings I allowed myself to feel during and after I let you in.

Don't go, don't leave, please

- Come back please do not leave me completely I still need you here beside me. Helping me through thick and thin. I still need a shoulder to lean on during the tough time. An ear to rant to when I am upset or feeling sad. I still want to tell you about my day and go into detail. I put my happiness in you, and I was a foul to do so. I stopped doing the things I loved, because I loved spending time with you more. Doing so I lost the love for those things because all I started to love was being with you. I still need you; I was not ready to let you go even though you were ready to let me go. Don't go, don't leave me here all alone in this cruel world. You said that we can live in this cruel world and fight it together. Please I still want there to be an us.

No right to love me anymore

- You left me and said you didn't love me anymore, then you come back and say you miss me and still love me. Hell, no you have no right to love me anymore. After you left me and said you no longer loved me, that there is someone else. I will not let you use me as a backup. I will not let you go around throwing shit on my name after you left me, then try and come back as if you did not do such thing. When I heard ever word you said after you left, when you think that I did not. You were there for me the relationship but not in the way we both know you should have been. You only listened when you wanted to you were only there when you felt like it and so much more. So, in the end it is a good thing you left and said you did not love me anymore. It is not a good thing you came back and said you still did though. I will not be as to so dumb to let you in all over again.

You're somebody else now

- From the person I knew a year ago to now. They are two completely different people. What happened to you like I made it clear you could always come to me for help or rant to me and I can try my best to help. You never reached out instead you're somebody else now. You are no longer the nice, kind, loving, and sweet person you used to be. You became mean, rude, hated, and overall different. I'm not judging you though because what ever happened to cause you to change that much I hope is better now. You had l light hair a year ago and now it is darker than ever. You always put effort into looking good, now you look like you just hurried out of the house. Do not get me wrong that is okay, but it is not just some days you look like that it is every day. Just like back then I am still here for you through thick and thin. I have your back against everyone who does not. I still love you no matter who you become.

Wasting all my tears

- I no longer have any more tears to cry. I sit in my bed staring at the ceiling or walls just trying to cry. I know I need to, but I wasted all my tears on you already. I cried so much I have no tears left in me to cry even when I am hurting so much that I can feel them in my eyes they just don't come out. I wasted all my tears on the pain I felt of you leaving, the way people judge me for feeling how I felt after the fact. I cried for so many of the same things I no longer can cry for anything at all. Not even the things I wasted all my tears on. I just need to feel okay and not like I am on the verge of tears, but nothing will come out. I know one thing for sure and that is I no longer will be wasting my tears on something or someone that is not worth it. I will no longer put my heart in that kind of pain, that it feels the need to cry constantly, because that drains my heart and breaks it in to pieces. That also causes my mind to never be able to slow down and just be silent. A mind that is a mess is reckless and causes enough pain. So, I refuse to let myself go through pain that causes me to want to cry, knowing I have no more tears in myself left to cry.

The words unsaid

- I wanted to say so many things when you left but I did not. Now I am left will all these words unsaid. Left wishing I could talk to you and say so much but I cannot because you left, and you want nothing to do with me. I also know that if I were to say anything you would go around and tell your friends then your friends would tell they friends and soon the word that I contacted you would get around. Then people would judge me and for what because I showed you that I miss you. I guess now a days people are not allowed to miss someone when they leave without being judged or criticized or just somethings. Making you feel as though you are not allowed to miss them, and no one likes that feeling, I personally do not. It sucks when someone's leaves and you do not get to say all the things you want to when they leave. That you only get to say a few things, that you must hide how you feel because you know you shouldn't say anything about it. When you know they will not care but telling them would make you feel better. The things is people say to put yourself first, but how can you do that when you know sayings all the words you want to would just makes things overall worse. To me words when a relationship ends never seems to make things any better only worse especially for yourself hearing what they have to say back to what you said. So instead, I will stay quiet and have all these words in my heart left unsaid.

Head in the clouds

- I always let my emotions cloud my judgment maybe it is because I have my head in the clouds too often, so I can never see things clearly. Either that or I see things to clear. I am the type of person to live off what if I did this, or what if this happened, or what if something bad comes out of this, I live by so many what ifs. Mainly because I see, by doing so I am protecting myself in away, because I have already thought of everything that could happen. By doing so I never live in the moment, instead I live in a head full of clouds. They are not good clouds they are sad they are gloomy, and they are dark. They are everything but good. I always tell myself get you head out of the clouds. When I hear head in the cloud, I think good things like I think of dreaming happy thoughts, thinking of happy things, but I do not feel that way when my head is in the clouds. I try my best to stop my head from being in the clouds, but I have lived this way for so long how could I stop now, why would I want to it has been one of the things in my eyes protecting me.

Take it easy on my heart

- I have been broken, I have been manipulated and used. I have been told so many lies by to many people. I have lost friendships and I have lost relationships. I have lost to many people to lose anyone else. All I ask is to anyone else who comes in my life is to please take it easy on my heart. I do not need it being broken more than it already has. After all it is just starting to heal so, please let it. I need comfort from my past friendships and past relationships. I do not need any more pain I need more happiness. So, if your intentions are to hurt me, please just leave, I have already been hurt enough. I have already been through enough with people I do not need anything more going on. I had to push people away and use up all my time to let my heart heal. I am sure some people know how that feels, it is draining and takes everything in you to stay busy, but in the end to me at least doing so healed my heart. Only because I never had time to stress or worry about things, only what I was doing to keep my mind off stuff. That was all the stress I needed during the times I was letting my broken heart heal. Anyways I drained myself and made myself absolutely exhausted to heal so please everyone do not put me through anymore that will cause me to do that all over again to stop my heart from breaking again or to cause my heart to heal all over again. Because doing it once was enough for me.

Before you and then with you

- Before you I was living life at my best and had only myself, I liked it that way. I thought I needed only myself, that I was the only person I needed in my life. I thought I could get myself through everything alone without anyone by my side, I thought that going through everything alone was easier than it ever could be with someone. I was sad and done with new people coming into my life. Then you came along and showed me it is so much better when you have someone by your side. Something about it is a feeling I stopped thinking I needed, now that I have it though I never want to let go. The things is I cannot completely explain the feeling yet. It could be because I am not used to it, or it could simply be because I am scared to admit these feelings to myself. The thing is I had been doing things on my own for so long I never stopped to think how it would feel having someone by my side. I could not be more grateful about how now I do have someone by my side. That I have someone to share my thoughts and feelings about rather than only my notes. That I have someone to listen and try their best to understand me. Someone who has yet to judge me for how I feel, best part is I never think they would. Because they have by far proven to me, they are with me through thick and thin.

Never be afraid to be you

- People will judge and always have something to say. The thing is you should not hide who you are for someone to like you or must be fake to feel as though you are good enough. You should be yourself no matter what, because if they do not like you for you why should you want them to like you at all. If you are afraid to be you then they are the ones that are not good enough, not you. Being you is what makes someone good enough. If you put up an act around people and not truly be yourself then no one will really like you, they will like the version of you that you created. I would never want someone to see me for who I am not or for who they want me to be, I would want them to see me for who I am and nothing less. You are who you are, and no one is the same as you, that is one thing that no can ever take from you. Unless you act as though you are someone else. Being who you are and unlike the rest is what makes you unique and what makes you stand out. No one is meant to fit in completely, we were all raised differently. We all have gone through different things that made us who we are. People have possibly gone through the same things yes, but they will never feel exactly how you felt. After all everyone feels things differently, along with sees things differently. At the end of the day do not be who people want you to be. Along with don't be afraid to show everyone the true you.

Something about you is like an addiction

- I love your smile, your laugh, I love your personality, your humor, your kindness, and so much more that I could go on and on about. Something about you is like an addiction and I cannot get enough of you, I love spending time with you, being by you, talking to you in person and through text. I love having you by my side through things and I also love being there by your side as well through things. I love how you make me happy, and I love how I make you happy. I love your warm and comforting hugs and I never want to let go. I love making you laugh because then I cannot help but laugh too. I love making small and big memories with you. I love the way you look at me. I love the way you smile at me. I love everything about you, but if I keep going on I will give in to the fact that I love you. Which I cannot do because love is a strong word, that I am afraid of using and afraid of hearing. So, when I feel that way, I just keep it in the back of my heart never admitting it.

If there is no fire, why sound the alarm

- If we are doing good and everything feel right why end it. Why make us nothings. If there are no problems and we are both willing to fight through things then, where are you going. Why are you sounding the alarms to stop us. I thought you thought there was no fire to put out. Like what happened there was no fire that I was aware of, or that you made me aware of. Did something happen you didn't tell me about or don't want to. There was no fire to put out we were good, things were great, we were perfect for each other. At least so I thought. You cannot just sound the alarms and not make me aware of why. I have the right to know and you owe me that much. I guess you do not think that though because you are gone now and there is nothing, I can do to stop the alarms from going off. I get it you stopped feeling everything you used to. The way you once felt for me is no longer there. I just hoped that when it ended, we could have still been friends.

People coming and going but they never stay

- I have had so many relationships it feels like, I mean I wouldn't count most as a relationship but still. I have had so many talking stages as well. For almost ninety percent of them they come back and leave again. The funny things is they all keep coming and going but they never stay. Why is it they cannot just stay for once, instead of just leaving and coming back. If anything, they all are just messing with my heart, and I am done with that. If you want to come into my life, you only get one chance at making me believe you will stay and only one chance to come back and make it worth it. I give no one more than a second chance when they chose to leave me. Because if someone can do it once they will do it again. I do believe people change, but not when it comes to finally deciding to stay. After all, if you wanted to you would have just stayed the first time.

Fall into me

- I am always there for anyone no matter what and I mean no matter what. So, if you need someone to talk to or someone to ramble onto about something I got you. It will stay between us, because it is not my place to tell anyone. If you need a shoulder to cry on, I got you. If you need arms to hold you come to me, I will hold you until you want me to let you go. If you have something none stop things on in your mind and you feel you cannot talk about it anyone, go ahead and talk to me if needed and if you want too of course. I will always be that person anyone can come to, does not matter if I know you or if I don't. Does not matter if I dislike you or like you. I am here no matter what. You can fall into me for advice and comfort. For closure and an ear to listen. Anything you need at all I am here. I will help the best I can and give my best advice or I can just listen up to you. I am none judgmental so whatever it is about I will not judge you or see you differently if anything I will see you as stronger for talking about it even when you were scared to. Those who talk to people about what they are afraid and scared to talk about are strong, they are not weak or pathetic they are everything but those words.

Save yourself

- When in a friendship or relationship that causes you more pain than it does happiness. You need to leave it and save yourself. If you are in any way like me. It will be so hard to leave because no matter how much bad people show you about themselves you chose to see the good. You chose to look for the best in everyone before you chose to see the bad. If someone is mentally destroying, you and it is taking everything in you to stay. Then you need to do yourself a favor and leave before you have nothing left to give. You can only see the good for so long before you must allow yourself to see the bad. If they are less worth it, then they are worth it you should leave. It is all your choice though. By doing so though you will feel relieved you no longer have to fight your gut when it is telling you they are not worth it. Always trust your gut most of the time it is right sadly that is the truth.

It took time

- Everything takes time in life. There is so many things in life that needs time. Time and effort are what makes everything happen. I have had so much time to get where I am at in life with myself and I am glad I took that time. The thing is I had a bad mind set back then and with time it got better. Back then I had a broken heart and with time the pieces got pieced back together. I had no energy for thing but with time I gained more. I stopped smiling and laughing but as time went on, I started smiling and laughing again. I lost so many people I never wanted to let anyone in again, with time I started to and some of them I regret others I do not. I thought nothing would ever be worth it, in time I started to think things were again. I stopped talking to people because I feared what they would say to me or how they would judge me, with time I started talking again and I stopped fearing what they had to say or if they would judge me or not. I stopped opening up about everything and anything, with time I started too again. I could go on about the things I accomplished with time. The things is though it is all your choice what you want to accomplish with your time. For me everything up above took time, there was a time I never wanted to change any of that stuff, but as time went on, I wanted to. Time is in your favor if you let it be.

Coping with pain

- Everyone who suffers with pain which is everyone. Has a different way of dealing with things. Which means you should not judge how someone chooses to do so. The best you can do is try your best to understand why they cope the way they do. I have had to many people in my life judge me for how I cope when I just needed someone to understand. Some people cope in good ways other people cope in bad ways. I see it as if they think it helps them with their pain they have ever right. Yes, choosing to do bad things is not a good way of coping, it is way. I have chosen to cope in bad ways, and here is why. I felt as though I had no one to talk to. That everyone I talked to would just judge me for what is causing me to cope the way I do, like most people have. So, I stopped talking about my pain and started coping in bad ways even worse than I already used to. I felt as though they would never really listen to me, or that they would stop being there for me after I tell them what is causing me to cope how I chose to. From my experience when coping badly I just needed that one person to be there no matter what, so if you know someone who copes badly. Just be there for them and try to understand them. One thing I know for sure is do not and I mean not tell them they need to stop, because chances are they know they need to stop, they are just not ready to. Chances are they have heard it enough and it only makes thing worse. Let people cope how they cope, and they can handle it from them, just be by their side. When they ask for help that is when you help do not force your way in.

Don't waste your time on the small things

- In my life I have focused way too much on the small things, then I remember they won't be there tomorrow. I have gone into way more detail than I needed about the small things and for what to try and make them big when deep down I know that they are not. Only making myself hurt more than I should about it. Everyone's idea of small things is different though, so never tell someone, that is a small thing. It could not be to them, or it could be, and they just will not allow themselves to admit it. Because if they do then they will know they just wasted their time for nothing, except for a small thing that could have been just done if they would have let it. I will not disagree that the small things can have the biggest impact on your life though. I know that the small things have had almost very close to the same impact the big things have for me. That is why I find it so hard not to waste my time on the small things. When the next day comes along you have the choice if you want to make the small things big or not. To make it easier on yourself I would say you should just let it go and move on, because it will not be there the next day. When it is not there the next day never let the small things come back start ignoring them and saving yourself from the pain you could feel over still feeling things over the small things. Every day is a new beginning in a way so make the best of it. Now I know me saying the small things in this paragraph did not really make sense it really does not to me. For some odd reason I feel as though the small things could mean whatever you would like it too.

Don't waste your youth on a broken heart

- I was young and I let getting my heart broken, take over my life. It caused me to grow up too fast. Mature faster than most people. I realized things I did not think I would when I was young. I grew stronger than I should have had to be. I was just a kid I was not supposed to be strong. I was supposed to be having fun and living my life to the best. Not constantly thinking about my broken heart. I pushed people away because I never realized back then that I was waisting my youth on my broken heart. I pushed them away because they never helped me, they made things worse. Now that I do see I wasted my youth on a broken heart, I wish I never let a boy make me feel the way I did. I mean now I know how to protect myself from feeling that way again. The things is though I should not have learned that at a young age. People called me dramatic for feeling how I felt, and I want to believe them now I do, but here is one thing I know it does not matter what age someone is if they are in pain about losing someone do not judge them, it only makes things worse. Be there for them and comfort them I don't care how you feel about the situation, how they feel should always come first. Speaking from experience. To those who judged me back then, guess what maybe when it was all over and dealt with. We could have laughed about it. Now whenever you bring it up all I feel is pain and remember every little detail that I no longer want to remember. So, the best thing I can ask for you to do is stop with bringing it up. Yes, I know I felt that way and I hate myself for it, but you do not have to make me hate myself even more by still bringing it up, it has been long enough it should just be in the past. Especially since I put it in the past, you should be able to as well, If I can do it, you can.

Feels like I am walking on ice

- One wrong step and I feel like I will break the ice and fall under and drown. That is how life feels now. Every time I say or do something I feel like I am walking on ice with what I said or did. Why though because it is not like I am saying anything bad or doing anything bad. Maybe it is just because I fear being judged for what I really have to say about something or what I really want to do. So instead of saying what I want to say I think before I speak and change it up, before doing what I want I stop and think about so many things that could happen. I always feel like I will break the ice. I do not want to fall back under ice again. I do not want to feel like there is no getting out so all that I have left to do is just drown they're underwater and in silence. Without anyone with me or anyone to help just me. Making it so I must help myself and get myself out from underneath the ice. I feel as though it is constantly breaking even if I am doing my best not to break it. I never feel like I am doing good enough. How I feel also breaks the ice, because if I am not feeling good emotions, I am walking harder on the ice then I should be. Life to me feels like walking on ice, one wrong move and I will go under. Then I will not be able to get back out and I will drown all over again, like I did back then. Which would explain why I still feel this way.

Killing me slowly

- Trying my best to do good at everything and anything I am doing in life right now is draining and I do not know how much more I have in me. How much more I have of myself to give to things and people around me. I know I am so close to just wanting to let it all out and go off, but I can't because if I do. I will be called too many different names. Back then when I got called names, I could not handle it, I have gotten better at it, and I have stopped letting what people have to say affect me. It still hurts though, knowing some people are so quick to judge and call people names. Knowing that some people only speak bad things about me. That they leave out the good. Like do not get me wrong I get it, I do the same sometimes. I admit though to the people that I am only speaking about the bad and not the good. So that they know there is good as well not only bad. I would never create a bad imagine of people, because in the end I only want what is best for them. So, when I say I do the same, I really do not. The thing is I do not know how much longer it will take me just to go off, I want to, but I know I will not. Because even though I get filled with rage sometimes because of myself, that does not mean I will take it out on others. I will say though that holding it in is killing me slowly. That I am drowning in all the bad things I am thinking of I cannot see through them at all to see the good things anymore. No matter what I will fight myself and see the good, no matter how much of myself I must give. I refuse to live thinking only bad things. Life does not feel worth it when I do that. I would like for life to feel worth it.

You were once

- There was a time in my life I thought you were what I needed to be happy. I thought that being with you was all I needed, and I did not need anything else. So, I put all my happiness in you. I was a fool to do so, because by doing so you broke me. I broke myself; I can see that now. You played apart, but I did the rest all on my own. You were once the person who put the biggest smile on my face, not anymore. When you left, I realized I was all I needed to be happy. That that only person I needed was myself. You made me realize I have enough strength in me to get through anything, all on my own. You taught me things I have been living by since you left, and I could not be more grateful for you leaving. Why you might ask well, because I found my worth in myself. I learned to love me, and I did not once stop to question myself, I started following my gut and I got somewhere in life, without you. Unlike I ever though I could, look at me now I did it. You were once the person I called the one. Now I know this might sound stupid, but I call myself the one now. I can do anything if I just put my all into it. I have myself and I will never lose me not anymore. Sure, at times I still will but it will no longer because of you that I do.

Never going to be the girl

- The girl I was back then will never be me again. I'm never going to be the type of girl who lets their walls fully down. I'm never going to be the girl who thinks she can talk about her thoughts. I'm never going to be the girl who believes someone one hundred percent, because I am just too scared. I'm never going to be the girl who opens up to people. I'm never going to be the girl who shows you who she really is. I'm never going to be the girl who does not feel like she is not being judged by people. I'm never going to be the girl who does not have anxiety and depression. I'm never going to be the girl who has never self-harmed. I'm never going to be the girl who is a good kid and has done nothing she should not do in life. I'm never going to be the girl who is content with the way she looks. I'm never going to be the girl who knows how to love and what it feels like to be loved. I'm never going to be the girl who does not over think things. I'm never going to be the girl who feels like she is enough. I'm never going to be the girl who someone stays with. I'm never going to be the girl who does not constantly think about her past. I'm never going to be the girl who does not live by expect the unexpected or that everything comes to an end.

I will explode soon

- No one understands this pain I feel, it is like I'm in pain, but I'm not. Everyone does not get it, I'm doing okay really, I am, but I'm not at the same time. I feel like a walking explosive. To many things get on my mind at once and I have no way of letting it all out. So, I feel as though I am going to explode. I can't talk to people, because then they get scared for me, feel sorry, or something. For one I can do it on my own, for two I have been doing it on my own for long enough, I can keep doing it. I just need to let it out to someone here and there so the explosion does not go off. I don't need you making me think I'm weak, because I know I am not I'm very strong. If you make me feel as though I'm weak, I'm going to stop talking about it and pretend to be okay, so you stop worrying. When I'm ready to explode at any moment now a days.

Don't say I can't handle myself

- I can to I have stayed alive when I feel as though I have been through hell and back. I have given my all for years, everything I have in me. Still to this day I do, when really, I feel as though I have nothing left in me to give. No matter what though I keep giving my all. I can handle myself I make mistakes, don't chose to just see my mistakes though. Don't see all the things I have done in pain, as bad or whatever you see it as. Because the thing is everyone makes mistake, everyone does different things when in pain. So, I'm sorry for making mistakes even though it is what people do. I'm sorry for the things I have done well in pain, even though I was not fully aware, because I was into much pain. Say I can't handle myself go ahead. It hurts though, because here is the thing at times I cannot, if you think I can't all the time we'll ouch. Everyone can't handle themselves here and there it is life. Do not make a huge deal out of it for me not being able to occasionally. It makes me feel as though you never think I can. I could go into so many reasons as to how I can handle myself. This just makes me way to mad. Hearing from someone very close to me say "I can't handle myself." Not just once, but repeatedly. That I cannot write about it any longer, then I already have.

My own way of words

- You know it is great because sometimes I can write like a poet other times I cannot. It is like at times my mind is running, and it can't stop, so I just write it all down. Other times it is blank, and I'm writing to feel something, but I don't really know what I am writing. On the days I know what I am writing and what I want to say, it is like poetry on days I don't know what I am writing or what to say it is not. I say it is nice being able to write so beautifully, and it is comforting. I guess when I had no one in my life to talk to about things I used my own words in my notes to get it out. I learned to comfort myself in a way I knew no one could by writing, I found something in me, I needed a way with words. I know I have always had my own way with words for advice and comforting people but until I started writing about my feelings in my notes or my experiences, I never knew I could use my own way of words for myself. My own way of words was all I had and what I learned to live with in a world where I felt I had no one. I had me and my own way of words and I couldn't have asked for anything more. Because my own words and I got me through thick and thin better than anyone else ever could. They still do so thank you past me for finding your voice in your notes. Because I needed that, and you found it, now it is something I will never lose. At least I know I have something to hold onto and that something is a part of me. That I will never let go, because that part of me saved me. No one else saved me I did and my own way with words. Not only does my own way of words help me it helps others.

I have been locked in a cage

- My mind and my heart have been trapped in a cage for so long, not letting out my thoughts and feelings to people. So here I am getting a book published. I feel so much better knowing there is a chance this could work. That I will finally have gotten to use my voice not completely, but in a way. To say what I want however I want without anyone being able to change what I said. That is all I need to finally get the key to my cage. Being able to unlock my heart and mind, for once. Being able to feel relieved for never being able to let my feelings truly out. Relieved for the fact I get to use my voice, to the fact I got to say what I want without anyone being able to change it, anymore.